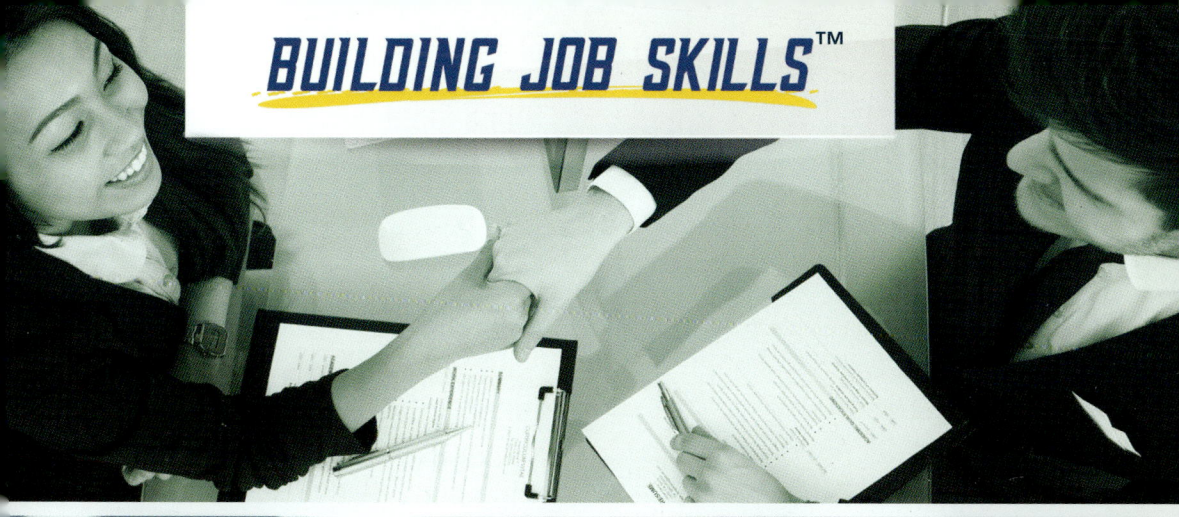

BUILDING JOB SKILLS™

ACE YOUR RÉSUMÉ, APPLICATION, AND INTERVIEW SKILLS

Elissa Thompson and Ann Byers

Rosen YA
New York

Published in 2020 by The Rosen Publishing Group, Inc.
29 East 21st Street, New York, NY 10010

Copyright © 2020 by The Rosen Publishing Group, Inc.

First Edition

All rights reserved. No part of this book may be reproduced in any form without permission in writing from the publisher, except by a reviewer.

Cataloging-in-Publication Data

Names: Thompson, Elissa, author. | Byers, Ann, author.
Title: Ace your résumé, application, and interview skills / Elissa Thompson and Ann Byers.
Description: New York : Rosen Publishing, 2020 | Series: Building job skills |
Audience: Grade level 7–12. | Includes bibliographical references and index.
Identifiers: ISBN 9781725347076 (library bound) | ISBN 9781725347069 (pbk.)
Subjects: LCSH: Job hunting—United States—Juvenile literature. | Résumés (Employment)—United States—Juvenile literature. | Applications for positions—Juvenile literature. | Employment interviewing—United States—Juvenile literature.
Classification: LCC HF5382.75.U6 T46 2020 | DDC 650.14—dc23

Manufactured in the United States of America

CONTENTS

INTRODUCTION 4

CHAPTER ONE
SO WHAT DO YOU WANT TO DO? 7

CHAPTER TWO
WHAT DO YOU HAVE TO OFFER? 14

CHAPTER THREE
CREATING A GREAT RÉSUMÉ 20

CHAPTER FOUR
MAKING THE INTERNET WORK FOR YOU 30

CHAPTER FIVE
APPLYING FOR JOBS 38

CHAPTER SIX
ACING THAT INTERVIEW AND GETTING THAT JOB 44

GLOSSARY 53
FOR MORE INFORMATION 55
FOR FURTHER READING 58
BIBLIOGRAPHY 59
INDEX 61

INTRODUCTION

So, what do you want to do with your life? You've probably been asked that question more than once. You've heard it from your parents, your aunts and uncles, your teachers, and even your friends. Deciding what you want to do with your life can feel like a gigantic, overwhelming decision. But it doesn't have to be that way. According to the Bureau of Labor Statistics, people will have more than eleven jobs in their lifetimes—and that is a number that's only growing. Millennials in particular are known for shifting careers or creating new jobs entirely. And no one knows yet what your generation will do.

Consider this: the internet was invented in the 1980s. Think about how much the World Wide Web has changed the world—and what kinds of jobs are available—since then. Today you can be a web designer, a social media manager, or even work on your laptop from your couch while your office is across the world. There is so much possibility and excitement for you as you begin to choose what you might like to do with your life.

The place to begin is with your first job. Getting out there and working is a great way to see what fits for you and what doesn't. But how do you go about finding a job? First you need to consider what you're good at, what you like to do, and what you have to offer. Maybe you want to talk things over with your parents or a teacher.

You have a great deal to offer as an employee, and there are so many different career paths you can take. It can be exciting to think about finding a great job.

Once you've decided on a potential career path, it's time to craft a résumé that will catch someone's attention. This will take time and care because, believe it or not, experts say human resources professionals take only six seconds to look over a résumé. As soon as those six seconds are up, they have moved on to the next potential employee. So how do you catch the attention of hiring executives? How exactly do you make them linger on a single piece of paper that sums up who you are?

There are many ways to make yourself stand out as you create your résumé and apply for jobs. Creating your résumé doesn't have to be a slog. By thinking about what you want out of a job, and a career, you can create a résumé and application that highlights the best that you have to offer. Remember, there is something special about you that is going to make someone say yes.

Once you nab an interview, you'll be ready to shine in person thanks to the hard work you did deciding why this job is for you. By knowing what you have to offer, you'll be able to let others know as well. With this groundwork done, your résumé proofread, and your interview aced, you'll be on your way to your very first career path.

Time to get to work!

Finding a job that works for you can be a great feeling. Working hard and earning money for yourself can make you confident.

CHAPTER ONE

SO WHAT DO YOU WANT TO DO?

Before you begin a job search, it's a good idea to take some time to think about what you might want to do as a career. Take ownership of the process and the path you would like your life to take. With some brainstorming and strategic thinking, you can find a job that you love. Think about what you like to do (your interests), what you are good at (your talents and abilities), and what is important to you (your values).

WHAT DO YOU LIKE TO DO?

How do you choose to spend your free time? If you had an afternoon to yourself, what would you do? Home in on your interests. Consider these questions and see what answers you come up with.

- Do you like to work with people or things?
- Do you want to work with your hands or your mind?

- Would you rather work with others or by yourself?
- Do you like to have a routine or to have things change a lot?
- Do you enjoy doing detail work or not worrying about the little things?
- Do you love to be outside or would you like to work indoors?
- Are you best with lots of activity around you or when things are quiet?

If you really love working with people, you will probably enjoy being a receptionist in a busy office, a server in a restaurant, or working in any number of other positions in which you can interact with the public. If you get excited about objects, you might prefer a job as a mechanic, a computer technician, a crew member in a warehouse, or working in some other place with equipment and machinery.

What areas of life seem interesting to you? Do you like technology, food, sports, or recreation? Do health, fitness, and the medical field appeal to you? Does business sound exciting? What about human services, like counseling or social work? Or public services, like police or firefighting? Could you spend all day teaching? Or do you see yourself building, designing, or making things?

You may be able to do a number of different things, but some of these things may rev you up while others seem to drain your energy. You will be happiest when you are in a field that you find exciting. Figuring out what you like to do will help you decide what kind of a job to look for.

THE POWER OF PERSONALITY TESTS

You have probably taken quizzes online to find out which Hogwarts house you would be in or what superhero you'd be, but have you considered taking a personality test to point you toward a career that's right for you? Consider asking your guidance counselor if your school has any tests that can help you. One popular test, the Myers-Briggs Type Indicator, can tell you a lot about yourself, like if you are an introvert or extrovert and how you think about things. Maybe you are intuitive and decide things with your gut. Or maybe you are a sensor and prefer to work with facts and data. Knowing these things about yourself can help steer you toward a career that's right for you. For example, if you're intuitive and an extrovert, maybe a job in a medical field could be right for you. You could see if any doctor's offices need help. If you're introverted and fact based, perhaps you might like to be a writer. You could try penning your own material, or see if a local author needs assistance. If you take the test, you can search the internet for your results and see what career types are suggested for you. See what feels right. You might discover something amazing!

WHAT ARE YOU GOOD AT?

What are you great at? Besides thinking about what classes you love at school, think about what your friends always ask you for help with. Composing emails? Styling hair? Editing pictures? Do you invent things? Do you like to argue and often win when you do? Are you the one who gets everyone together for

When thinking about what kind of job you want to get, consider what you like to do in your free time. What activities do you like to do with your friends? Is there a job equivalent?

a party or project? Are you good at taking care of people? Can you explain complicated things in simple terms? Do you have an eye for fashion? Do you keep careful records? Are you a great driver? You probably have many talents that you have not thought of yet.

Beyond your natural talents, you have abilities you have gained through practice. Not everyone has musical talent, but most people can learn to play the piano. If you are interested in something, you can develop an ability to do it well. Your talents and abilities are important not just in finding a job to apply for, but also in getting that job and excelling at it. These are the assets you have to offer an employer.

WHAT DO YOU CARE ABOUT?

Jobs are about earning money. You are doing a task in order to get a paycheck. But there are so many types of jobs available to you. Take a moment and consider the things that matter most to you. These are the things you might want to prioritize when looking for a job. You want a position that works with you—not against who you are and who you want to be as a person. Look over this list of work-related values. What matters most to you?

- Helping others
- Influencing others
- Being independent
- Doing something meaningful
- Expressing yourself
- Being in charge
- Having adventures
- Receiving recognition or prestige
- Expressing creativity
- Having security
- Being in a low-stress environment
- Moving around a lot

Pick your top three and make sure any job you apply for is a good match.

Do you love helping other people? Perhaps the health care field would be a good fit.

STARTING YOUR JOB SEARCH

You have thought about what you want out of a job, what you're good at, and what you can bring to a position. It's time to start job searching. What to do first? You can certainly begin by searching job sites on the internet. Use what you've learned about yourself to look for jobs that would be a good fit and are of interest to you. A word of caution, however. Because online listings are easy to find, lots of people are looking at them besides you. This means that jobs listed online can be harder to get because so many people are applying for them. A recent article in *Forbes* magazine states that only about 4 percent of people find a job via online listings.

Another place you can try to look for work is via social media. The Pew Research Center reports that 43 percent of young adults (ages eighteen to twenty-nine) have used social media to look for a job. Follow places you might be interested in working at on social media, and see if they post any job openings.

These strategies can be a great place to start. But you also might want to consider asking your mom for help. Really. Your friends and family are a great way to find out about job opportunities. By asking people you already know—and the people they know— about positions at places you're interested in working, you are more likely to get a job. Laura Smith-Proulx, who has helped many people get high-paying jobs in big companies, says asking about positions even when none are advertised is a good way to find a great job.

So What Do You Want to Do?

Searching for jobs online can be a great way to start your employment hunt. But make sure you are looking for positions in other ways, too. There are many ways to find a job.

If you have a career goal, look for work in that area. You may need more education to reach your dream job, but you might find a beginning position in the field. For example, being a clerk in a floral shop could be the first step to a job as a flower arranger. These entry-level jobs also give you a taste of what a higher-level job in the same field might be like. They help you find out how well you like the career you are considering. They also give you experience and contacts that make it easier to apply for your next position.

CHAPTER TWO

WHAT DO YOU HAVE TO OFFER?

Now you have an idea of what you'd like out of a job. It's time to think about what you have to offer. Before you write your résumé, it's good to get organized. Think about what you've done and how you can present it to get where you want to go. To get the job you want, you need to think like the person who will hire you. The three top things most employers look for are a good attitude, dependability, and skills. Do you have those qualities? How can you show an employer that you are the one who should get the job? You must prove that you are what that employer wants. Take some time to organize all the information you can use to sell yourself.

SCHOOL

Your education suggests what you can do. Maybe you have not accomplished a particular task, but you know how to do it because you have been trained. Think about more than the schools you have attended.

What Do You Have to Offer?

As a young person looking for a job, no one expects you to have a lot of experience. Describing your schooling will help employers get a sense of your attributes, what you have learned, and your skills.

Have you had any special training related to the job you are seeking? Did you take any classes that gave you work-related skills, like computer training, auto mechanics, woodworking, or photography? Did you attend any workshops while you were involved in extracurricular activities such as peer counseling, student government, or school newspaper? Write all of this down with the dates of your schooling. You can also add your projected graduation date, and your GPA if it is impressive. This information will become part of your résumé.

WORK HISTORY

An important part of your résumé is where you list your work history—in other words, jobs you have done before. If you haven't had an actual paying position before, don't worry. First off, as a teen no one expects you to have had a full career already. You have done things that are worthy of your résumé, you just need to think beyond traditional paying positions.

Imagine a girl named Lisa. She's never held a job before, but she helps her mom out a lot with her younger sisters. She takes care of them when her mom has a meeting or when her dad has to work late. She volunteers at her church and is involved with the annual rummage sale that raises money for kids in need. She also helps as a counselor in training at a summer camp. These are all great items to put on a résumé. They show she is responsible and caring, two great attributes.

Here are some things for you to consider as you prepare your résumé. Are you involved in sports, clubs, or other activities in school? Do you have hobbies? What school projects did you complete or help with—building a model, making a video report, raising funds? Have you participated in community outreach such as painting fences or homes, distributing food to needy families, or cleaning up neighborhoods? What responsibilities do you have at home? Write down everything you can think of that you have done.

Do you know how to code? Are you fluent in HTML? Are you social media savvy? These skills can all help you land a great job.

SPECIAL SKILLS AND MORE

You know what you're good at, your accomplishments, and what you've achieved at school. This should all lead you to your skills. Your skills can be quantifiable, like computer programs you can use and if you have customer service experience. They can also be more abstract in nature, like the fact that you're a team player. You can list that you are flexible, organized, or punctual.

REFERENCES

All the information in your résumé comes from you. It paints a picture of you. Employers usually want to know how other people see you, too. So they ask for references. You can be one step ahead by having references ready for when your potential employer asks. Do you know people who would be glad to recommend you for a job? They could be teachers, coaches, or people you have worked or volunteered with. Your parents or relatives do not count as references because they can be seen as biased on your behalf. Ask your potential references, in person if possible, if they would speak on your behalf if a potential employer contacts them. Then, if you know they will be getting a call from a potential employer, you can contact them (email is fine) to give them a heads-up. Send them the job listing or let them know about the position so they can better speak to your experience and why you'd be a good fit.

When you have organized the information that will go into the picture you will paint of yourself for a prospective employer, you are ready to write a great résumé.

MYTHS & FACTS

Myth: If you didn't get paid for something, it doesn't count as work experience.
Fact: Helping around the house, volunteer work, and more can count as work experience on your résumé. "A lot of students overlook the value in the things they do, like taking care of younger siblings," said Matthew Moor, a college-and-career pathways coordinator, told Catherine Gewertz at *Education Week*. He said teens "work in their communities, but don't correlate it with leadership. It's those daily things they don't think of as important or worth mentioning."

Myth: The best way to find a job is by applying to online listings.
Fact: According to Matt Youngquist, the president of Career Horizons, there are more effective ways to look for work. Youngquist told NPR, "At least 70 percent, if not 80 percent, of jobs are not published. And yet most people—they are spending 70 or 80 percent of their time surfing the net versus getting out there, talking to employers, taking some chances [and] realizing that the vast majority of hiring is friends and acquaintances hiring other trusted friends and acquaintances."

Myth: It's a good idea to put a photo of yourself on your résumé.
Fact: Images do not belong on résumés. Many résumés go through application tracking systems that analyze your résumé for certain keywords. An image can cause the software to malfunction, which may mean your résumé gets discarded without ever being seen. So keep the pics to yourself.

CHAPTER THREE

CREATING A GREAT RÉSUMÉ

Crafting a great résumé that showcases your talents is an important part of finding a job.

Now you know what kind of job you want, and you know what you've done that might get you hired. You found a listing to apply for, or you heard about an opening that might be a great fit from your mom's best friend. What's next? You've got to write your résumé. Creating a résumé can seem like a scary prospect, but it doesn't have to be. All you are doing is summing yourself up on a single sheet of paper.

In writing your résumé, you must think like the person who will be reading it. Employers may have a lot of résumés to read, and they read them very quickly. They are not reading them to get to know anyone; they are reading to see whom they can eliminate. Your résumé has to show them, within seconds, that you are able to do the job.

YOUR 411

Start off your résumé with your name and contact info. Give your potential employer all the best ways to contact you: your email address and phone number (cell is fine, just be sure to answer it and check your voice mail). If your email address is based on a funny nickname or a joke, you may want to get a new one that features your name. What might employers think if they try to reach you at something like babyface@hotmail.com? Look at everything on your résumé the way a prospective employer would. You can include your mailing address if you would like, but it is not necessary. If you have a professional website or social media handles that will speak to why you should have the job you are applying for—say you are applying to a bakery and your Instagram is full of pictures of cookies you baked—add them, too. If your social media is just pics of your friends having fun, you can leave it off.

SUMMARIZE YOURSELF

Here's where all that thinking about what you are good at and what you want out of a job will come in handy. On a beginner's résumé, many people include an objective, which tells the hiring executive what, exactly, you're looking for. Some examples from Monster.com:

- "To obtain an entry-level [industry] position at a respected organization and utilize the educational qualifications I've obtained at [name of school]."
- "To gain employment at [specific company], which will inspire me to enhance my skills in [specific industry] and work as a team player in a positive atmosphere."
- "To obtain an entry-level position as a [specific job title] that will allow me to utilize the skills gained at [name of college or university] and build a long-term career in [specific profession]."

Your job objective should be specific. If you are applying for different jobs at different companies, prepare a separate résumé for each one, and change the objective to reflect the specific job you are applying for.

EDUCATION

Next up is your schooling. Because you probably don't have a lot of work experience yet, it's a good idea to list your education first. List the name of your school, its city or town, and state. This is where you also list impressive coursework that relates to the job you are applying for, your GPA if you would like, and your graduation year.

WORK, SKILLS, AND MORE

You've gathered all the info on your accomplishments, your previous jobs, volunteer experience, and more. List them out, with the dates you did them. List the places you have worked, starting with your current or most recent job, and go backward. Give the dates you worked, the name of the company, and the job title. Under each listing, describe two or more achievements. Begin each with an action word such as "developed," "presented," "organized," or "planned." Verbs are more powerful than nouns, and you want your accomplishments to sound strong. Next up, list your skills. List the skills that the job calls for and, under each skill, describe your accomplishments in that area. Think about the accomplishments you brainstormed.

CHOOSING A STYLE

So you know what should be on your résumé, but what should it look like? If you search the internet, there are many templates and format examples available for you to try. Whether to use a template or not is up to you. Some people advise against it, saying your résumé should reflect who you are, so you should create it from scratch. The main thing to keep in mind is making sure your résumé is easy to read, for both the people and software that will encounter it. So if you do choose to use a template, select a very simple one with a focus on the words, not fancy design elements.

Ace Your Résumé, Application, and Interview Skills

Choose a format that reflects who you are, but that is also easy to read. Remember that your résumé should scan easily so application tracking software can process your information.

If you choose to create your résumé yourself, set the page with one-inch margins all around. If your résumé ends up being too short, you can increase the margins later. Choose a standard font, such as Times New Roman, Courier, or Ariel. Nothing fancy. Do not use more than one type of font. Point 12 is an easy-to-read size. If you go much larger, it looks as if you do not have much to say and are trying to fill empty space.

Begin with your name and contact information. You can center this or set it flush left (every line even with the left margin). Make your name stand out by putting it in boldface. You might also use a slightly larger font or type your name in all capital letters. Below your name,

Creating a Great Résumé | 25

A compelling cover letter can help you land an interview. Be concise and convincing while making a case as to why you're the best person for the job.

on separate lines, type your mailing address if you want to add it, phone number, and email address.

Next you will place the Objective, Education, Experience (or Relevant Skills) sections. To make each section easy for the reader to find, put the titles in boldface and leave spaces between sections. In a short document, titles that are flush left are generally easier to spot than titles that are centered.

Within each section, use short phrases or sentences to talk about yourself. Employers want to get to the point quickly, so leave out any unnecessary words. Beginning each phrase with a bullet gives a sharp look and organizes the items nicely. If your bulleted items are not sentences, do not put a period after them.

SAMPLE RÉSUMÉ

JOHN DOE
111 Main Street
Cleveland, OH
(555) 555-5555
jdoe@email.com
johndoe.com

Objective: To work as an auto parts clerk, utilizing skills gained in mechanics class.

Education
Roosevelt High School, Cleveland, Ohio
Classes in auto mechanics

Work Experience
Bob's Burgers, Cleveland, Ohio, 2016–present
- Wait on customers
- Cook and prepare food orders in fast-paced environment
- Advanced from cook to assistant manager in 18 months

Car Repairperson, Cleveland, Ohio, 2016–present
- Perform minor repairs and tune-ups
- Rebuilt engine of Ford Mustang

Skills
Knowledgeable in diagnostic skills and relevant software

WRITING A GREAT COVER LETTER

When you apply for a job, in addition to sending your résumé, you also need to write a cover letter. This letter more specifically explains why you are right for the position you are applying for. A cover letter, usually sent via email, is a business communication, so you should use a professional tone. Write the letter like you are addressing a respected adult in your life, like your school principal. Do not use any slang or emojis. Be yourself, but professional.

If you can, try to find the name of the person doing the hiring. You can call the company and ask for the name. Make sure you have the correct spelling. Even a common name like Smith can be spelled more than one way. If you cannot find the name, address your letter to the Personnel Manager or Hiring Director.

A cover letter can look very simple. The first paragraph says that you are writing to apply for a particular position. It can mention how you heard about the opening. The second paragraph highlights your qualifications for the job. These qualifications will be on your résumé, but your cover letter should go into more detail. A good tip is to write this paragraph as if you are explaining to your friend why you are perfect for the job. Write about what makes you right for the position. The last paragraph asks for an interview. Getting an interview is what your cover letter is all about.

Ace Your Résumé, Application, and Interview Skills

SAMPLE COVER LETTER

Here is what a sample cover letter would look like:

Dear Personnel Manager:
I am writing to apply for the position of [insert job title here].

[Paragraph detailing why you are right for this role. Take examples from your résumé and expand upon them. Explain more fully why they should hire you specifically.]

I would like the opportunity to talk with you about this position. I believe I would be a great fit in this role.

Sincerely,
Your Name
jdoe@email.com
(555) 555-5555

Proofreading is an important part of finalizing your job-hunting documents. Make sure to read everything over carefully—twice!

PROOFREAD—AND THEN PROOFREAD AGAIN

After you write your cover letter and résumé, print them out and read them over carefully. Is the punctuation correct? Are all the words spelled correctly? Don't rely on spell-check. Both "skill" and "spill" are words, but if you want people to know you are experienced in several types of painting, you don't want them to read that you have "a variety of paint spills." See if any spaces are uneven and how the formatting looks. When you are satisfied, ask other people to read it and tell you honestly what they think. If you make any changes, read the entire document over again.

Take a moment to congratulate yourself. Putting together a résumé and cover letter is hard work, and you did it! You're on your way to finding a great job.

CHAPTER FOUR

MAKING THE INTERNET WORK FOR YOU

You've got your cover letter and résumé done. You're applying to job listings and asking friends about positions. What else can you do to make yourself stand out? The internet, of course!

WHAT'S THE MAGIC WORD?

Application tracking software has changed the way human resources professionals hire for new positions. The computer program scans submitted résumés, looking for keywords that are related to the job opening. Then the program selects the most-qualified candidates, and those are the ones then considered for interviews. So how to make sure you get noticed? Read the job listing carefully, and try to incorporate the words used there throughout your résumé. If a job wants "customer service experience" and you have this, make sure to write it on your résumé in this way. Word it the same way, and always spell out abbreviations. This means you might have to make an individual résumé for every job, but it is worth it if you get called in for an interview.

THE PROFESSIONAL ONLINE YOU

You might already spend a lot of time online. In addition to searching for job listings, there are other online activities that can help you get a job.

ONLINE PORTFOLIO

If you have decided on the type of job you want to get, consider creating a personal website that explains further why you are right for this career path. Start by searching online for portfolios of other people who are already established in the field you would like to break into. Study these websites, their layout, and the information included. This way you can get an idea of what your website should look like and the terminology you should use.

Let's say you're an artist who wants to get into graphic design. You might have done some cool projects, at school and during your extracurricular activities. You might even have work you've done on your own. You've looked up other graphic designer portfolios and have an idea of what you should include. Gather your materials, just as you did to write your résumé. Then get started on creating a website to showcase your work. It doesn't have to be anything fancy. You can use online templates to build a simple website highlighting your work.

Your website should have a few pages. A main page, with a short headline that sums you up. This tagline does not need to be as formal as your résumé objective. Then there should be an About Me page that talks about who you are and why you love design. Your bio doesn't have to get into specifics about where you go to school or other parts of your life. Focus on your chosen field and what makes you stand out in that particular arena.

Next up should be a page called Work or Art, or something similar. Here you could feature some of your pieces, maybe with short descriptions of their creation. Finally, a Contact page should list your email address. Have someone proofread your website just as they would your résumé and cover letter. Once you are pleased with how your website looks, add the URL to your résumé, under your email address, at the top. Let people see all the hard work you've done.

GETTING LINKEDIN

LinkedIn is a professional networking site where people use their résumés as their profile pages. While lots of adults use this website to network and find new positions, kids as young as thirteen are allowed to join as well. You do not have to get a LinkedIn page, but it is something to consider if you do not want to create an entire website for yourself. LinkedIn can be a good way to keep track of your skills and accomplishments. Get a friend who's great at taking photos to take a professional-looking headshot of you. Wear business clothes.

Making the Internet Work for You | 33

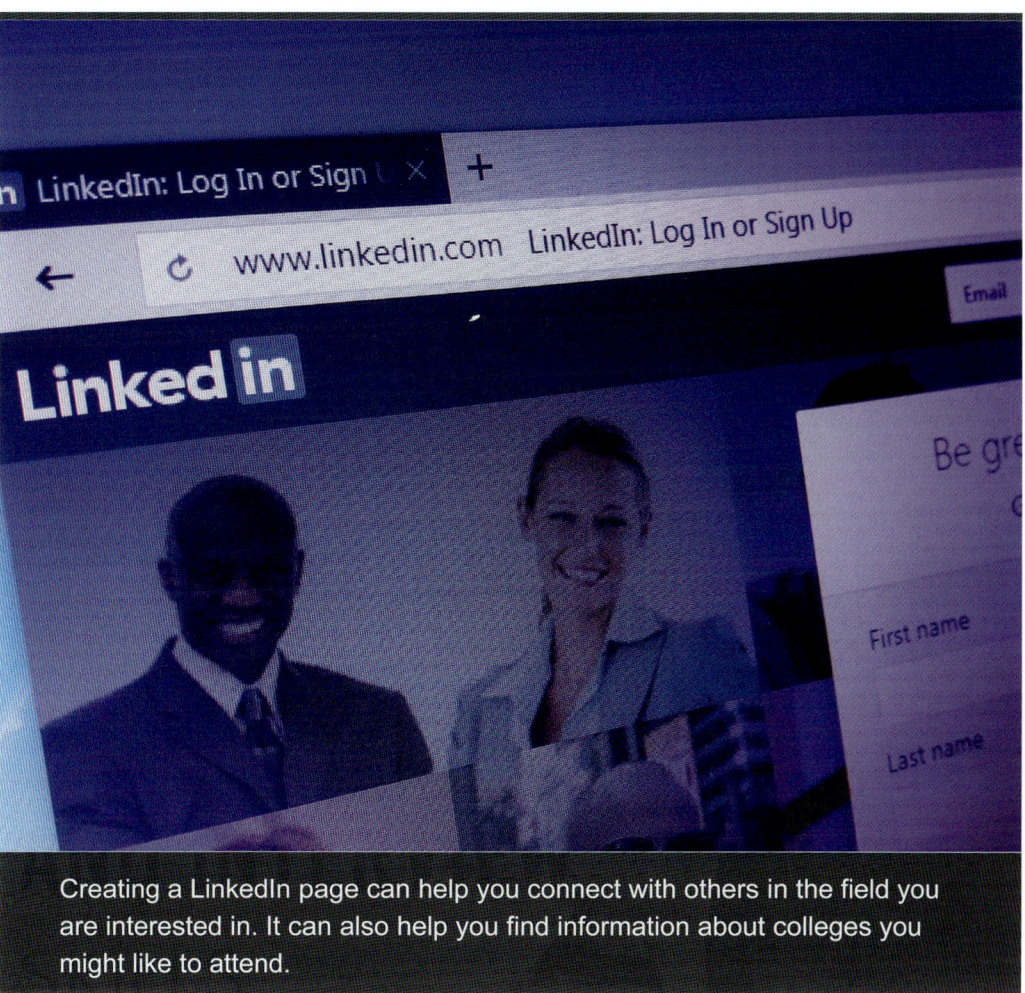

Creating a LinkedIn page can help you connect with others in the field you are interested in. It can also help you find information about colleges you might like to attend.

If you do decide to create a LinkedIn page, talk it over with your parents first to make sure they're okay with it. Keep a close watch on your privacy settings. You can make your page private or public, follow others in a field you are interested in, and more. Just remember, like all social media, you have to be careful when using it.

INTERNET SAFETY 101

You've heard it before, but it's so important that it bears repeating: never reveal personal information on the Internet. That means you should not post your home address or your cell phone number. If you decide to put your résumé online or if you create a website showcasing your skills, the only contact info you need to provide is your email address. If someone does contact you about a job, let a parent or trusted adult know, and look the person up. Never meet someone in person whom you've communicated with only online without fully vetting them and talking with an adult about it. Your safety is important.

THE POWER AND PERIL OF SOCIAL MEDIA

Social media helps connect you to those around you, near and far. It can be a great way to keep in touch with your cousins who live across the country. It can be fun to post pictures of your friends at that 5k you ran. It can also help you find a job. You can follow people or organizations you might want to work with in the future, even interacting with them from time to time. But this means you have to act professionally and not post anything that might make someone think twice about hiring you. According to a report from the Pew Research Center, 2 percent of social media

Making the Internet Work for You | 35

Social media can be a great way for you to connect with companies you're interested in working for. It can also help you develop your brand. But, as always, it's important to be careful and mindful when online.

users reported that they didn't get a job they were applying for because of what they'd posted online. So use caution. Think before you post. Be respectful of others—and yourself.

BUILDING YOUR BRAND

You've probably heard people talk about their brand before. But what, exactly, is your brand? "My own simple definition: A personal brand is how you are perceived by the outside world," wrote Daniel Decker for *Forbes.* "Therefore, personal branding is taking control of that perception and shaping it into whatever you'd like it to be."

Another writer for *Forbes,* Susan Gunelius, put it like this:

> Branding yourself is just like branding a product line or business. The same principles that marketers use to create brands like Nike, Campbell's, and Honda apply to personal branding. Consider women like Oprah Winfrey and Martha Stewart. Both of these women have defined their personal brands, created a brand image, message, and promise, and continually meet the world's expectations related to their personal brands.

For example, Meghan loves beauty products, especially nail care. She often does amazing manicures for herself, her family, and her friends. She even creates new colors by combining products. To develop her personal brand, Meghan should begin documenting her work—because it is work—on social media. She can start an account dedicated to her love of nail care. She can post pictures of her amazing manicures, share tips and tricks, maybe even make videos of how she creates designs. This social media account will mostly consist of nail care posts. Meghan should not post pictures of her friends out at a party on this account. This is her work account, to help build her brand. She can gain followers and follow others who share her love of manicures. Then, if she would like to apply for a job at a salon, Meghan has a whole portfolio ready to share.

As a member of iGen, you know more about growing up with the internet than anyone else. By thinking carefully and planning, you can use your internet skills to help you get a great job.

CHAPTER FIVE

APPLYING FOR JOBS

Your résumé, cover letter, and website are all set. There's another piece of the puzzle to consider as well. The job application. Most companies have their own application form, but some items are fairly standard. Learn what these items are and write down your responses to them. Take the paper with your responses—consider it a "help sheet"—when you are job hunting. That way, you will be ready to fill out an application easily and quickly.

BEING PROFESSIONAL

In addition to the help sheet you will prepare, you might have other papers to bring while applying for a job as well: copies of your résumé, your list of references with their contact info, and examples of the work you have done. If you put them all in a hard-sided folder or notepad, you will keep them neat and clean. Besides, when you come into an office or business carrying a nice notebook, you look much more professional

Applying for Jobs | 39

THE IMPORTANCE OF PENMANSHIP

Some applications are online, and you can type your answers. But some applications you will have to fill out on the spot. Which means you need to write neatly. Be careful and go slow. You don't want to cross a lot of items out and hand in a messy application. Read the instructions carefully. If they say to use black ink, do not use blue. If they say to print, then print. If they say, "Do not leave any space blank," fill in everything. Remember, an application is a screening tool, and a poorly filled out application will screen you out. Take your time. You are ready for this.

A job application is different from a résumé and cover letter. Be sure to bring all your info so you can fill out an application on the spot if you need to.

than if you pull a folded piece of paper out of your pocket. How you look is just as important as how your application looks!

YOUR 411

- **Personal information**. In addition to your name, you will need your Social Security number. You may have to give your driver's license number and proof of citizenship. It is a good idea to have these identification cards with you in case the person receiving your application wants to attach copies. Along with your address, you might be asked how long you have lived at that location. If it is less than a year, you might have to give the same information for the place you lived before your current address. Write all of this down on your help sheet.
- **Position name**. Companies often use one application for many different jobs, so the application may ask what position you are applying for. Give the exact name of the job if you know it. Sometimes an application asks how you heard of the opening, so have that information with you,

You'll need your Social Security number and other personal info when applying for a job, so be prepared.

too. Be as exact as you can. If you saw an ad online, write down the name of the website.
- **Salary requirements**. You may see a line for "salary requirements." Like all the other items, this is a screening question. You don't want to be screened out by giving a figure that is too high, but you don't want a job that pays too low. If you can, research the company or the type of job to get an idea of what people are getting paid in that position. If you cannot find out anything definitive, you can write "open" or "negotiable."
- **Physical limitations**. Applications often ask if you have any physical conditions that limit you in doing certain kinds of work. If you say yes, you are not automatically screened out. It is illegal to deny you a job because of physical disabilities.
- **Education**. Applications often ask for names of the schools you attended (high school and above), the dates you attended each, and whether you graduated. Sometimes they want your grade point average (GPA) and the number of credits you earned. If you received a General Educational Development (GED) certificate instead of a diploma, you can give that information. Be prepared to list any certifications you have and the dates they were issued or the dates they expire.
- **Experience**. Applications generally have space for you to list all of the jobs you have had for the past five years or longer. In addition to the names and addresses of

companies, the titles of the positions, and the dates worked, make sure you have the names and phone numbers of your supervisors on those jobs. Also be ready to write down the amount of money you were paid. If the item says "earnings per _____," you decide whether to put how much you earned per year, per month, per week, or per hour. You might want to have the figure for each on your help sheet.

- **Moving on**. Employers want to know why you left or are considering leaving another job. Try to express your reasons for leaving in a positive way. Remember, employers want

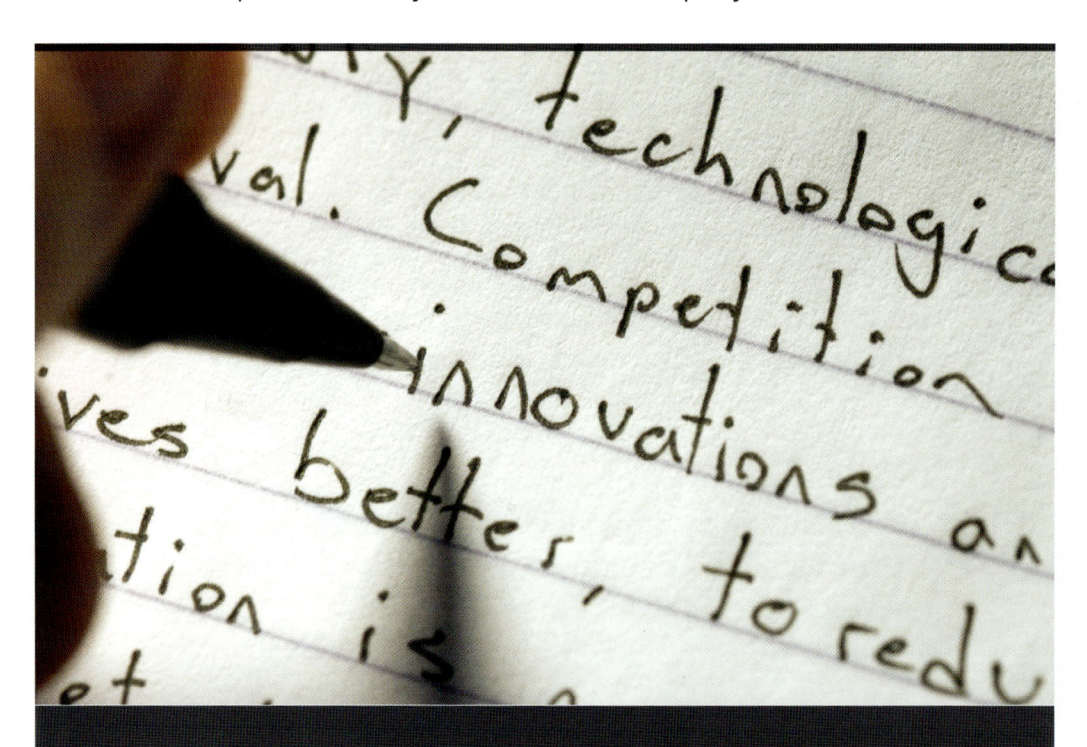

Use neat penmanship when filling out an application. You want your potential employer to be able to read your information, right?

people with good attitudes. You might say (if these are the real reasons) "to seek a more challenging opportunity," "to find full-time work," or "to explore a different field."
- **Past employers**. Employers deciding whom to hire may want to call your previous supervisors. They want to know how dependable and skilled you are. They also are trying to find out how well you get along with other people. However, they also understand that you may not want your current employer to know that you are looking for another job. So where the application asks, "May we contact your present employer?" it is perfectly all right to write no.

When you are finished filling out the form, read it over again to make sure it is clear and accurate. The interview is the next step!

CHAPTER SIX

ACING THAT INTERVIEW AND GETTING THAT JOB

You did it! You scored an interview. This is a big deal and you should be proud of yourself. Now you need to go in and show why you're the best person for the job.

DRESS PROFESSIONALLY

It is important to look professional when you go into an interview. Think of an interview as a special occasion and dress up. That means no tank tops, flip-flops, or sneakers. Wear a suit. Or slacks and a button-down shirt are OK, too. Consider adding a tie and a jacket or sport coat. A plain dress or a simple skirt with a nice blouse can also work. It's a good idea to leave off the perfume or cologne, or at least go lightly—your interviewer could be allergic to certain odors. And consider popping a breath mint in your mouth while you are waiting for the interviewer to call you in.

Acing That Interview and Getting That Job | 45

Dressing professionally for an interview is a great way to show that you are serious about this employment opportunity. Show your potential employer that you care.

DO YOUR RESEARCH

To make sure you will be on time, plan how you will get there. If you are going by car, drive the route ahead of time so you know how long it takes. Plan alternate routes in case your way is blocked. If you will be taking a bus or another form of public transportation, make a practice trip a day or two before. Whether you are going by car or public transportation, try to do your dry run at the same time of day you will be traveling for your interview. Traffic can be different at different times of the day. You don't want any surprises. Just in case something you can't imagine happens and you are late, you should have with you the name and phone number of someone at the company.

Look up the company that has called you in. Make sure you know about the business, any new initiatives they might have, and with whom you will be speaking. Taking some time to research the company can help show that you are really interested in the position.

The night before your interview, get everything ready. Iron your clothes, shine your shoes, and organize your folder or notepad. You will want to have extra résumés, your list of references, and the help sheet you completed. Make copies you can leave with the interviewer; do not give anyone your originals.

ACT LIKE YOU DESERVE THIS JOB—BECAUSE YOU DO!

Be sure to arrive early. "On time" for an interview means ten minutes before it is scheduled to start. You will feel nervous, but remind yourself that you can do this job.

Acing That Interview and Getting That Job | 47

You are happy to finally have the chance to convince your prospective employer that you can do it. You look great, you are prepared, and you are eager to show the interviewer who you are and what you can do. Thinking like this will help you feel confident, and interviewers like confident people.

Three actions say you are confident: smiling, making eye contact, and giving a firm handshake. When you smile, you look like you are happy to be at the interview. When you look the interviewer in the eye, you show that you are not afraid of him or her. And a solid handshake makes you appear strong. These three simple actions go a long way toward making a great first impression.

Interviews can be scary but by preparing ahead of time, you can keep those nerves away. You got an interview because you deserved it, so be confident.

MOCK INTERVIEW

It's a good idea to practice some common interview questions ahead of time. You may be asked, "What is one time you overcame a difficult situation?" This is a tough question to answer on the spot. While at home, come up with a good answer. Generally, try to put past experiences in a positive light, if you can, while still being honest: "It was difficult, but it taught me to be more assertive." Turn your negatives into learning experiences. Other common questions include: Tell me about yourself. What is one of your greatest strengths? What is one of your greatest weaknesses? Why did you decide to apply for this job? Why do you think you're right for this position?

The interviewer will give also you a chance to ask questions. You should ask two or three because if you have no questions, you will appear uninterested in the job. Do not ask about salary or vacation. Those questions can make an interviewer think you do not care about anything else. The time to ask about pay and time off is when you are offered the job.

Throughout the interview, take your cues from the interviewer. Stand until the interviewer sits or invites you to sit.

A seemingly silly but very real concern is what to do with your hands. Hand movements can betray nervousness and they can be distracting. One way to take care of this issue is to bring something with you that you can hold. Remember the folder or notepad you use for keeping copies of your résumés? Bring that and add paper and pen for taking notes.

Acing That Interview and Getting That Job | 49

Always write a thank-you note after an interview. Email is perfectly fine and quick, but dropping a handwritten note in the mail can be a nice touch.

THE IMPORTANCE OF THANK-YOU NOTES

As soon as you leave the interview, write a letter to the interviewer. Thank the interviewer for taking time to consider you for the position, and repeat your qualifications for the job. Email it right away. You can consider sending a handwritten thank-you note that you send via mail as well. Then wait. Give the employer five to ten days after receiving your

It can take some time, but you will find a job. By being patient, persistent, and working hard on your skills, an employer will soon choose you.

thank-you letter. If you do not hear from the employer in that time, you can email to say you are checking on the status of the position opening. And then you may have to wait some more. Spend your waiting time exploring other job openings.

Do not get discouraged if you do not get an interview right away. Do not be frustrated if you are not offered a job after a great interview. Remember that getting a job is as much work as having a job. Polish your résumé, practice your skills, and keep at it. Your hard work will eventually pay off!

10 GREAT QUESTIONS
TO ASK IN AN INTERVIEW

1. Ask something specific about the company, showing that you took the time to learn something about it.
2. How would you describe this company?
3. What job duties will I be responsible for?
4. What would a typical day in this position be like?
5. What would a typical week in this position be like?
6. What one thing would make a person most successful in this position?
7. What one thing should I know about this position?
8. What is the most challenging part of this position?
9. How do you measure success?
10. What do you like about this company?

GLOSSARY

application tracking software A computer program that analyzes résumés for keywords, selecting the most qualified to send to the next round.
asset An item, ability, or quality that has value. A person's talents, skills, education, and experience can be assets to an employer.
bias Favoring one thing or person over another. Often considered unfair.
brand An identity or image created to be convincing to others, usually through marketing or promotion.
bullet A graphic device used to designate items in a list. A bullet is usually a dot, and it is placed at the beginning of each item.
cover letter A letter that is sent with a résumé or another document introducing the document. When job applicants send résumés to a prospective employer, they should send a cover letter with each one.
entry-level Refers to a beginning job in any field, a job that does not require much skill or knowledge.
extrovert A person who is outgoing, often friendly and talkative to many people.
flush left Even with the left margin of the paper.
human resources The department or employee handling hiring, workplace complaints, firing, and other personnel issues.
introvert A person who is quiet in groups and sometimes considered shy.
keyword A word or phrase employers look for on electronic résumés. Keywords are usually words that describe a job applicant's skills or experience.

margin The border of a document or similar object.

negotiable Something that is up for discussion, capable of being changed.

objective Something one works toward, a goal.

prospective employer A person who is not your employer now but who may become your employer in the future.

relevant skills Abilities that have to do with the job for which you are applying.

salary The amount of pay one receives for work done. Often paid by a monthly or yearly rate.

template A preset form that is used to create a document.

FOR MORE INFORMATION

Career OneStop
(877) US2-JOBS
Website: https://www.careeronestop.org/
Facebook: @CareerOneStop.org
Twitter: @Career1Stop
A US Department of Labor website that contains job listings, information on job skills, application help and more.

Career Professionals of Canada
(866) 896-8768.
Email: info@CareerProCanada.ca
Website: http://careerprocanada.ca
Search job openings, listen to podcasts, learn about employment strategies, and more from this Canadian association.

Job Futures: Canada's National Career and Education Planning Tool
Service Canada
140 Promenade du Portage, Phase IV
Hull, QC K1A 0J9
Canada
(800) 622-6232
Website: http://www.jobfutures.ca/en/home.shtml
The Canadian government offers job hunting resources, including listings.

Myers & Briggs Foundation
2815 NW 13th Street, Suite 401
Gainesville, FL 32609

Email: coordinator@myersbriggs.org
Website: https://www.myersbriggs.org/home.htm?bhcp=1
Learn about the popular personality profiler and how figuring out who you are can help you decide on a career.

National Career Development Association
305 N. Beech Circle
Broken Arrow, OK 74012
(910) 663-7060
Website: https://ncda.org
Facebook: @NCDACareer
Instagram: @ncdarg
Twitter: @NCDAwebeditor
Find career resources like interest assessments and information about different occupations, professional development opportunities, and salaries.

South Carolina State Library
1500 Senate Street
Columbia, SC 29201
(803) 734-8666
Email: reference@statelibrary.sc.gov
Website: https://guides.statelibrary.sc.gov/c.php?g=82003&p=528699
Find video tutorials, reference links, job advice, and more to assist with finding employment.

US Bureau of Labor Statistics (BLS)
US Department of Labor
Postal Square Building
2 Massachusetts Avenue NE

Washington, DC 20212-0001
(202) 691-5200
Website: http://www.bls.gov/home.htm
Twitter: @BLS_gov
The BLS is the main fact-finding agency for the US government in the field of labor economics and statistics. On their K–12 page, you can learn about different occupations through games, quizzes, Q&As, and more.

YouthJobs Canada
999 Canada Place
Vancouver, BC
V6C 3E2
(800) 383-8060
Website: http://youthjobscanada.ca
Facebook: @Youthjobs Canada
Twitter and Instagram: @youthjobscanada
This organization is dedicated to helping Canadians aged fifteen to twenty-four find work.

FOR FURTHER READING

Catherman, Erica. *The Girls' Guide to Conquering Life: How to Ace an Interview, Change a Tire, Talk to a Guy, and 97 Other Skills You Need to Thrive*. Grand Rapids, MI: Revell, 2018.

Cuban, Mark, Shaan Patel, Ian McCue, and Mark Cuban. *Kid Start-Up: How You Can Be an Entrepreneur*. New York, NY: Diversion Books, 2018.

Leavitt, Amie J. *Becoming a Project Manager*. New York, NY: Rosen Publishing, 2018.

Middleton, Angela. *How to Get Your First Job and Build the Career You Want*. St. Albans, United Kingdom: Panoma Press, 2015.

Pelos, Rebecca. *Cool Careers Without College for People Who Love Shopping*. New York, NY: Rosen, 2018.

Pelos, Rebecca, and Greg Roza. *Cool Careers Without College for People Who Love Writing and Blogging*. New York, NY: Rosen Publishing, 2018.

Rauf, Don. *Getting Paid to Manage Social Media*. New York, NY: Rosen Publishing, 2017.

Rauf, Don. *Strengthening Portfolio-Building Skills*. New York, NY: Rosen Publishing, 2018.

Spilsbury, Louise. *Got Career Goals?: Skills to Land Your Dream Job*. New York, NY: Enslow Publishing, 2018.

Thomas, Isabel, and Greg Foot. *Fantastic Jobs and How to Get Them*. Oxford: Oxford University Press, 2018.

BIBLIOGRAPHY

Bloch, Deborah. *Get Your First Job and Keep It*. New York, NY: McGraw-Hill, 2002.

Boles, Richard N. "The 10 Best And Worst Ways To Look For A Job." *Forbes,* September 5, 2016. https://www.forbes.com/sites/nextavenue/2016/09/05/the-10-best-and-worst-ways-to-look-for-a-job/#6d0021592e7b.

Bureau of Labor Statistics. "Number of Jobs, Labor Market Experience, and Earnings Growth Among Americans At 50: Results From A Longitudinal Survey." US Department of Labor, August 24, 2017. https://www.bls.gov/news.release/pdf/nlsoy.pdf.

Decker, Daniel. "Four Steps to Taking Control of Your Personal Brand." *Forbes,* October 30, 2018. https://www.forbes.com/sites/forbesagencycouncil/2018/10/30/four-steps-to-taking-control-of-your-personal-brand/#4bf9ad451b02.

Farr, Michael. *Getting the Job You Really Want*. Indianapolis, IN: JIST Works, 2002.

Farr, Michael. *The Very Quick Job Search: Get a Better Job in Half the Time*. Indianapolis, IN: JIST Works, 2004.

Gewertz, Catherine. "What I Learned From Helping Students Build Résumé and Interview Skills." *Education Week,* February 13, 2019. https://blogs.edweek.org/edweek/high_school_and_beyond/2019/02/what_i_learned_from_helping_students_build_resume_and_interview_skills.html.

Gunelius, Susan. "Define Your Personal Brand." *Forbes,* March 12, 2010. https://www.forbes.com/sites

/work-in-progress/2010/03/12/define-your-personal-brand/#20dae4cd49f4.

Kaufman, Wendy. "A Successful Job Search: It's All About Networking." NPR, February 3, 2011. https://www.npr.org/2011/02/08/133474431/a-successful-job-search-its-all-about-networking.

Mahoney, Sarah. "8 Job Search Tips for Teens." *Family Circle,* June 2010. https://www.familycircle.com/teen/jobs/job-search-tips-for-teens.

McKay, Dawn Rosenberg. *The Everything Get-A-Job Book.* Avon, MA: Adams Media, 2007.

Miller, Marissa. "How to Write a Résumé When You Don't Have Job Experience." Teen Vogue, November 15, 2017. https://www.teenvogue.com/story/how-to-write-a-resume-when-you-have-no-job-experience.

Miller, Marissa. "7 Résumé Tips for Your First Job." Teen Vogue, February 26, 2018. https://www.teenvogue.com/story/resume-tips-first-job-search.

Monster.com. "Entry-level Résumé Objective Examples." Retrieved March 24, 2019. https://www.monster.com/career-advice/article/entry-level-resume-objective.

Morgan, Hannah. "How To Write A Good Resume for Applicant Tracking Systems." *U.S. News & World Report,* February 25, 2019. https://money.usnews.com/money/blogs/outside-voices-careers/articles/how-to-write-a-good-resume-for-applicant-tracking-systems.

Smith-Proulx, Laura. "Effective Job Search Techniques: Expanding Your Reach Beyond the Internet." May 22, 2007. http://phoenix.jobing.com/blog_post.asp?post=4560.

INDEX

A
abilities, 7, 10–11
application, 6, 38, 39, 40–41, 43
application tracking software, 19, 30
applying for jobs, 6, 10–11, 12, 13, 19, 20, 21, 22, 27, 28, 30, 34–35, 36–37, 38–43, 48
attitude, 14, 42–43

B
brainstorming, 7, 23
brand, personal, 35–37
bullets, using, 25
Bureau of Labor Statistics, 4

C
career, 6, 7, 9, 13, 16
  building, 22
  goals, 13
  path, 5, 6, 19, 31
  shifting, 4
confidence, 47
cover letter
  finished, 30, 38
  proofreading, 29, 32
  sample, 28
  writing, 27

E
entry-level jobs, 13, 22
extrovert, 9

G
guidance counselor, 9

H
human resources professionals, 5, 30

I
interests, 7, 8, 10
  and companies, 46
  and jobs, 12
  and social media, 12, 33
internet, 4, 30, 37
  job exploration on, 9, 30–37
  safety, 34
  searching for jobs on, 12
  searching for résumé templates on, 23
interview
  acing, 6, 44–51
  arriving for, 46
  asking for, 27
  conduct during, 47, 48
  confidence during, 47
  dressing for, 44
  getting an, 6, 27, 30–31, 43, 44, 51
  mock, 48
  preparing for, 46
  ten great questions to ask in an, 52
  thank-you notes and, 49
  traveling to, 46

introvert, 9

J
job search, 7, 12–13

K
keywords, 19, 30

L
LinkedIn, 32–33

M
margins, 24
medical field, 8, 9
mock interview, 48
Myers-Briggs Type Indicator, 9

O
objective, 21–22, 25, 26, 32

P
parents, 4–5, 18, 33, 34
penmanship, 39
personal information, 34, 40
personality tests, 9
physical limitations, 41
portfolio, online, 31–32, 36
professional dress, 32, 44
proofreading, importance of, 6, 29, 32
prospective employer, 18, 21, 47

Q
qualifications, 22, 27, 49

R
references, 18, 38, 46
relevant skills, 25
research
  interview-related, 46
  salary, 41
responses, on applications, 38
résumé
  copies, 38, 46, 48
  creating, 5, 6, 20, 23, 24
  finished, 30, 38
  images on, 19
  information on, 18, 19, 21–22, 27, 28, 32
  on LinkedIn, 32
  online, 34
  polishing, 51
  proofreading, 6, 32
  sample, 26
  scanning, 30
  separate/individual, 22, 30–31
  style, 23
  time spent reading, 5, 21
  what to send with, 27
  work history on, 16
  writing, 14, 18, 20–21, 29, 30, 31

S
salary
  asking about, 48
  requirements, 41
sample résumé, 26
school, 9, 14–15, 22, 26, 32, 41
  achievements, 17

activities, 13, 16, 31
classes, 9, 13
skills, 14, 15, 17, 22, 23, 25, 26, 29, 32, 43, 51
internet, 37
website to promote, 34
social media
job searching via, 12
manager, 4
power and peril of, 33, 34–35
your presence, 21, 36
style, for résumé, 23–25

T

talents, 7, 10–11
teacher, 4, 18
templates, 23
online, 31
thank-you notes, 49, 51

V

values, 7
work-related, 11

W

work history, 16, 23, 26, 41–42

ABOUT THE AUTHOR

Elissa Thompson is a journalist who has been published in *USA Weekend*, the *Baltimore Sun*, and *In Touch Weekly*, among others. She received her master's degree in journalism from the University of Maryland. She has written and edited several other books for Rosen Publishing. She got her first job at an ice cream shop at fifteen, thanks to a referral from a friend.

As director of a youth program, Ann Byers has examined résumés, conducted interviews, and hired people for a variety of management, entry-level, intern, and volunteer positions. She has coached young people through the entire job search process and has written résumés as well as interview questions. Byers knows what employers look for and how to show them you have it!

PHOTO CREDITS

Cover (foreground) sirikorn thamniyom/Shutterstock.com; cover (background top and background center right), pp. 1 (top and center right), 7, 14, 20, 30, 38, 44 (background top and background center), 39 Andrey_Popov/Shutterstock.com; cover (background center left), p. 1 (center left) © iStockphoto.com Weedezign; cover, pp. 7, 14, 20, 30, 38 (background bottom), p. 1 (bottom) NicoElNino/Shutterstock.com; p. 5 Pattanaphong Khuankaew/EyeEm/Getty Images; p. 6 Sarah Fix/DigitalVision/Getty Images; p. 10 KaptureHouse/hutterstock.com; p. 11 Monkey Business Images/Shutterstock.com; p. 13 Pixsooz/Shutterstock.com; p. 15 Cynthia Farmer/Shutterstock.com; p. 17 iinspiration/Shutterstock.com; p. 20 (inset) © iStockphoto.com/RossHelen; p. 24 Sirinarth Mekvorawuth/EyeEm/Getty Images; p. 25 (inset) peepo/E+/Getty Images; p. 28 Lamai Prasitsuwan/Shutterstock.com; p. 33 Stanislau Palaukou/Shutterstock.com; p. 35 mama_mia/Shutterstock.com; p. 40 Mega Pixel/Shutterstock.com; p. 42 Jamesmcq24/E+/Getty Images; p. 45 © iStockphoto.com/Koji_Ishii; p. 47 Nick White and Fiona Jackson-Downes/Cultura/Getty Images; p. 49 JaniceRichard/E+/Getty Images; pp. 50–51 Speedkingz/Shutterstock.com.

Design and Layout: Michael Moy; Photo Researcher: Sherri Jackson